## The Effective DRE:
## A Skills Development Series

# Maintaining Professional Balance

## BY DR. CHARLOTTE PRATHER

## RICHARD REICHERT
## SERIES EDITOR

**NATIONAL CONFERENCE FOR
CATECHETICAL LEADERSHIP**

LOYOLAPRESS.
CHICAGO

**NATIONAL CONFERENCE FOR CATECHETICAL LEADERSHIP**

3021 Fourth Street, N.E.
Washington, D.C. 20017-1102
1-202-636-3826

# LOYOLAPRESS.

3441 N. ASHLAND AVENUE
CHICAGO, ILLINOIS 60657
(800) 621-1008
LoyolaEducationGroup.org

## Acknowledgments:

The Scripture quotations contained herein are from the *New Revised Standard Version Bible: Catholic Edition*, copyright © 1993 and 1989 by the Division of Christian Education of the National Council of the Churches of Christ in the U.S.A. Used by permission. All rights reserved.

Excerpt from *The Wounded Healer* by Henri Nouwen, copyright © 1979 by Image Books, a division of Doubleday. Used with permission.

Excerpts from the English translation of the *Rite of Christian Initiation of Adults*, copyright © 1985, International Committee on English in the Liturgy, Inc. All rights reserved.

Excerpt from *The Way of Faithfulness: Contemplation and Foundation in the Church* by Padraic O'Hare, copyright © 1993 by Trinity Press International. Used with permission.

Excerpts from *The Documents of Vatican II* (Abbott-Gallagher edition) reprinted with permission of America Press, Inc., 106 West 56th Street, New York, NY 10019. Copyright © 1966. All rights reserved.

Excerpts from *Guidelines for Celebration of the Sacraments with Persons with Disabilities*, copyright © 1995 United States Catholic Conference, Inc., Washington, D.C. Used with permission. All rights reserved.

Excerpt from the *Holman Bible Dictionary for Windows*, copyright © 1994 by Broadman and Holman Publishers, Nashville, TN.

Cover Design: Shar Coulson Design

Copyright © 1998 by The National Conference for Catechetical Leadership, 3021 Fourth St., N.E., Washington, D.C. 20017. Phone: 1-202-636-3826. All rights reserved.

ISBN: 0-8294-1053-8

Printed in Canada.
04 05 06 07 08 Webcom 5 4 3 2

# Table of Contents

# About This Series

The Effective DRE: A Skills Development Series has been developed by the National Conference for Catechetical Leadership (NCCL) to help DREs and those preparing to become DREs to acquire the basic competencies required to be effective in the ministry. We recognize that the term DRE will mean different things in different dioceses throughout the country. We use the term DRE here as broadly as possible and intend it to refer to anyone involved in or planning to become involved in a leadership capacity in a parish religious education program. The actual scope of the leadership position can range from responsibility for the total program to responsibility for a particular portion of it, such as the task of serving as the coordinator for a junior high or senior high program. Thus the booklets, though addressed specifically to DREs, are designed to be of assistance to all parish catechetical leaders regardless of the title assigned to them or the scope of their job description.

The material in the booklets is based on the *National Certification Standards for Professional Parish Directors of Religious Education*, a document developed by the NCCL and approved by the United States Catholic Conference Commission on Certification and Accreditation. The *Standards* document is quite extensive and identifies and explains a wide range of skill and knowledge areas. We did not attempt to cover all of them in these booklets. Instead we used two criteria in deciding what topics to develop.

First, we sought to identify some of the most essential skill/knowledge areas, namely those most needed by anyone in a catechetical leadership position (such as recruiting and training volunteers or developing a program). Second, we sought to identify topics where information is not as readily available. For example, topics like knowledge of Scripture, theology, or expertise in the areas of catechetical methodology and conscience formation, though clearly essential to any catechetical leader, are topics about which much has already been written. So we chose instead to offer help with other important but less frequently discussed topics (such as budgeting and keeping records or maintaining personal balance).

Authored by experienced DREs and religious education professionals, the booklets provide practical advice, proven methods, and specific procedures for carrying out the many essential tasks related to directing a parish religious education program.

The series can be used as a resource in a formal diocesan ministry training program or in a small group study program. It can also be used by an individual for self-study. The entire series provides a comprehensive study program. Or, since each booklet is self-contained, persons may study only those booklets dealing with the skills they wish to improve.

Finally, the booklets can be kept on the DRE's resource shelf to be referred to whenever help is needed in carrying out a particular task.

# Introduction

This booklet is about something all of us find challenging: balancing our personal, professional, emotional, and spiritual lives. The subject is not a scientific one. Much can only be learned by experience. Colleagues and friends are the best allies anyone has in ministry and in life. Most of the good and sane things I know have come from these life-giving human relationships. Moreover, I think it can be taken for granted that anyone who is reading this booklet is involved in the ministry of religious education because of that central relationship we have with the God of wonder and surprises.

All the work we do has its origin, development, and end in the Spirit within us all. May all who read these pages find in them humor, a source of hope and optimism, and some encouragement on a path blazed by the apostles and enlightened by the Lord Jesus.

# 1 The Vocation of the DRE

The daily work of the parish director of religious education is much like the elephant that a group of blind men tried to describe after each approached it from a different angle. One, grabbing the tail, thought it was a rope. Another, seizing the trunk, thought it was a snake. A third, feeling its side, thought it to be a wall. Grasping its leg, another thought it was a tree, and the last, grasping its ear, thought it was a fan. A DRE's work looks different from each person's perspective. For the DRE, it looks different every day of the week, every liturgical season, with every new pastor, every new change of staff—sometimes every hour. We are teachers, and teachers of teachers, but also counselors, advocates for social change, spiritual directors, Scripture scholars, and theologians. We may find ourselves in the role of liturgical choreographers, leaders of song and games, mediators, and even cooks. Sometimes we pick up trash and weed gardens on our rounds of the parish. We are often expected to be experts on canon law, sacramental guidelines, Catholic social teaching, doctrinal matters of every kind, child development, principles of pedagogy, group dynamics, and budgets. We are expected to keep abreast of the latest publications, as well as with music and video materials for a great variety of educational needs. We should be acquainted with the people and programs of the pastoral offices of our dioceses, avail ourselves of educational opportunities, provide our volunteers with opportunities for spiritual nurture and continuing education, and maintain a network of connections with our colleagues at other parishes. We must be able to address the whole parish on occasion and to listen with quiet compassion to each person who crosses our threshold.

None of us do all of the above all the time. None of us do all of the above equally well, nor with equal enthusiasm. But none of the above remains totally outside the experience of any DRE for very long. The variety of tasks is so overwhelming that in the end it is hard to say exactly what this elephant really looks like. Although job descriptions vary from place to place, typically the DRE has the general oversight of educational programming within a parish.

Most often the focus of this ministry is religious education for children, including preparation programs for first reconciliation, Eucharist, and confirmation. It is common, however, for the DRE to have responsibility for many other areas as well: adult education, catechumenate, Scripture studies, sacramental preparation programs for marriage and infant baptism, parish evangelization, faith-sharing groups, preparation of Masses with children, and children's liturgy of the Word.

Education is certainly the common thread of the many tasks of the DRE. It is important to understand the nature of education that is specifically religious. Religious education is truly educational, but it is not academic. Rather, it is evangelizing, contemplative, and formative. Its goal is the development of informed Christians, with the emphasis more on Christ coming to light within each person than on any information we may provide. That is to say, all information imparted in the course of religious education is in the service of Christ, making Christ known and loved, helping others know that through their baptism they have put on Christ, bringing Christ to light in others. For DREs, this transformation in Christ must also persist in ourselves.

At the copy machine, in the classroom, or in the staff meeting, we need to be mindful of this reality: At the center of our work is Christ. That is why this chapter is entitled "The Vocation of the DRE." Our work is a work to which we are called by God. Our response springs from the grace of our baptism, and involves saying "yes" and receiving the gift with open hands and great joy. Our ministry to people must be, first and foremost, a witness to and a reflection of God's abundant love.

## EVANGELIZING

The work of the DRE is *evangelization*. Whatever doctrinal concepts are to be presented, the primary content of religious education remains a proclamation of the Good News. For the most part, the work of the DRE is with baptized people and, therefore, in theory at least, with people who are already evangelized. The experience of many Catholics, however, may reflect an initial evangelization that is only partial and inadequate. These Catholics may know doctrine but do not have a lived sense of God's salvation in the context of their daily lives. The reality of the DRE's work today will also include the unbaptized— older children and adults who participate in the renewed catechumenate process of the Rite of Christian Initiation of Adults (RCIA). There will also be families in the parish with interfaith marriages, where the religious education process is challenged to share the Gospel with fervor while respecting and honoring the sincere religious faith of non-Christians. Finally, there will be many opportunities for evangelizing those who have become alienated from the practice of Catholicism. In their pastoral letter *Go and Make Disciples*, the bishops of the United States stress this fundamental call to proclaim the Gospel: "Evangelization is the central mission of the Church" (p. 2). If this is so, then evangelization is the central work also of the DRE.

To be an evangelizer, DREs must attend to their own ongoing need for conversion to the Gospel, to what *Go and Make Disciples* calls "our continued receiving of the Gospel of Jesus Christ, our ongoing conversion both individually and as Church" (p. 3).

Attention to evangelization that is ongoing means that we will put the story of Jesus as told in Scripture and as met in our lives at the head of our projects. We will be doing the normative practice of the catechumenate: "breaking open" the Word of God. Our first step, before we can speak to another, is to listen and hear the Word proclaimed. Then we can witness to it and live it. We may ask three simple questions: What did I see or hear? What does it mean? How do I live it? Our reflection on these questions is revelatory—both when we apply it to the Scripture we have heard and when we ask it in life's unfolding drama. What do I see, hear, touch, and witness? Where do I discern Jesus in each event, person, and situation? Where is the Good News here? How do I live it now? Asking ourselves these questions will bring us back to the central focus around which all our ministry revolves—the person of Jesus Christ.

## CONTEMPLATIVE

This understanding of evangelization in the work of the DRE leads us to the second important quality of religious education today. Religious education is *contemplative* education. By "contemplative" I mean simply being open to see, hear, touch, taste, and attend to all that is. Being contemplative means being willing to set aside expectations so that we can notice something new, because the Gospel is good news. It means we take time to gaze on and listen to the God who is self-revealing and whom we meet in Scripture and sacrament, in nature and art, in others and in our own hearts. And it means helping others to do the same—to attend to the reality of their own religious experience, to recognize it, to reflect on it, to trust it.

The challenge of this contemplative understanding of religious education is to develop what Barry and Connolly call a "contemplative attitude" (*The Practice of Spiritual Direction*, pp. 46–64). A contemplative attitude of mind and heart is one that remains present to what is happening now. We look at our students, our colleagues, our own body, mind, and spirit. We become aware of God in ordinary things and in not-so-ordinary people. We listen to God speaking within us, and we revere God present in the lives of others. We notice God animating the Church. This does not imply a Pollyanna attitude that denies the existence of problems, conflicts, or sins. It does mean a willingness to be present to the mix and the messiness of human society, the universal Church, and the local parish.

For the busy DRE, a contemplative attitude can be a life- and sanity-saver. We will be reminded that the interruptions of the day are as real as our long-term projects. If we are open to the prospect of being surprised by God, no task, however trivial or tedious, will be exempt from the realm of that graceful surprise. This is an attitude we cannot transmit to others by indoctrination but can share with others through our stories, our behavior, our very way of being in relationship with them.

The stories of our faith—the Bible—and the stories of our Church—the lives of saints and sinners—are perfect vehicles for facilitating the development of a contemplative attitude. In those stories, only ordinary in the sense that all our lives are ordinary and only extraordinary in the very same sense, we and those whom we serve will discern the presence of God. In those stories, all of the content of faith is revealed, beginning with the very life of the Trinity, which penetrates and informs the community of believers.

In a wonderful book on contemplation, education, and faithfulness, Padraic O'Hare points to the fruits of a life lived in contemplative awareness:

> . . . a fundamental psychological posture of gratitude moment by moment, reverence for themselves and others and each evolving moment, that is, reverence for time. Only the contemplative being can resist violence; only the contemplative being has the resources to create hospitable social environments in which this reverence, rather than violence, is lived.
> —*The Way of Faithfulness: Contemplation and Formation in the Church*, p. xiv

## FORMATIVE

The title as well as the whole thesis of O'Hare's book suggest the third dimension of religious education I want to highlight. Religious education is *formative*. It is oriented toward forming Christians—people who live in a way that identifies them as followers of Jesus. We do not receive the faith, we are not evangelized, we are not baptized for our own benefit. Nor do we pass on the faith, evangelize, and baptize others for their own sake as individuals. The Church exists not to save itself but for the salvation of the world. Each person's baptism moves all of humanity and all of creation a little closer to the kingdom of God.

The work of religious education in the parish, the work of the parish DRE, is then the formation of Christians. We need to actualize our faith in concrete moments of service to the world. We need to take seriously the story in John 13 of Jesus washing the feet of his apostles. If those of us who commit our time and energy to ecclesial ministry were to receive a towel and pitcher, along with our desks, phones, libraries, and computers, we might perceive in that symbol an inkling of our true calling. We live in a self-reliant society. As Jesus did, we might find that our friends do not want to have their feet washed by us. Likewise, we too may be uncomfortable as recipients of another's humble service. But if we are to retain our energy and sense of humor in the face of so many responsibilities, we need to sit down for a while and let the Lord wash our feet, and perhaps also, along with Peter, our heads as well. Our contemplative attitude will give us the eyes to notice the Christ who comes in an unexpected guise to serve us or to challenge us to move beyond ourselves in service.

It is said that in the early Church, when the catechumenate first flourished, the bishops would ask questions of the community about the readiness of catechumens. The community was asked whether those seeking Christian initiation had faithfully helped people in need, especially the widows and orphans of the community. Today we ask: "Have they faithfully listened to God's Word proclaimed by the Church?" "Have they responded to that Word and begun to walk in God's presence?" "Have they shared the company of their Christian brothers and sisters and joined with them in prayer?" (*Rite of Christian Initiation of Adults*, #131 B). In these questions are contained the evangelizing, contemplative, and formative dimensions of authentic religious education. Those about to be elected by the bishop have experienced the proclamation of the Word, have listened to it, have entered into a prayerful relationship with God in the company of the Christian community, and have begun to live the Word that they have heard.

It would be a grave oversight to assume that our work is complete when our religious education processes and programs result in a conceptual understanding of the faith. Mental comprehension is only the beginning of the mission of the DRE. Our teaching must flower into a lived relationship with God in prayer and obedience, and a fruitful love for neighbor, evidenced by genuine community, concrete acts of service, and a commitment to structures of justice and peace. Sadly, we often look only at intellectual comprehension when we speak about education.

The text of the RCIA speaks of the elements that constitute "appropriate catechesis" for the period of the catechumenate. The catechesis provided should be liturgical and "solidly supported by celebrations of the Word." It should lead to "a profound sense of the mystery of salvation," to prayer, to the theological virtues of faith, hope, and love. The catechumens are "to practice love of neighbor, even at the cost of self-renunciation." They are seen as having "set out on a spiritual journey." They are transformed into "a new nature made perfect in Christ," a transformation that is gradual and progressive, becoming "manifest by means of its social consequences" (#75ff.). The DRE needs to take account of such appropriate catechesis in order to be an effective agent for authentic religious education in the parish.

We need to ask ourselves: Do I hear the Word? Am I celebrating it? Do I see and listen to Christ in the Word proclaimed or read, studied, witnessed, taught? As a result of this ministry, am I growing in faith, hope, and love? Where is this growth evident in my life? Do I see myself, along with those to whom and with whom I minister, on a spiritual journey? Is transformation gradually taking place in me? Do I see Christ in myself, in the events of my life, in my work? In my encounters with students, parents, volunteers, colleagues, and family, am I practicing love of neighbor? Is there any self-renunciation about my way of relating to all these people? Am I aware of the social consequences of my way of life and work? This list of questions is not intended to discourage or depress but rather to alert the DRE to the real action of God in his or her life. If we are not aware of all the good news present in our ordinary affairs, we are missing the Lord whom we have set out to proclaim. This is not an invitation to pride or self-righteousness but rather an affirmation of God's gifts, real and present in ordinary ways every day. We need to notice them, nurture them, and live in joy and gratitude because of them.

## VOCATION

This chapter began with the notion of the work of the DRE as a vocation, a calling from God. It is, therefore, not our choice but God's choice of us that has set us on this path. We can keep before our eyes the words of Jesus:

> I do not call you servants any longer, because the servant does not know what the master is doing; but I have called you friends, because I have made known to you everything that I have heard from my Father. You did not choose me but I chose you. And I appointed you to go and bear fruit, fruit that will last.
>
> —John 15:15–16

These words can be a source of reflection for this vocation of ours.

In reflecting on these words of Jesus, M. Basil Pennington writes: "I call you friends, because I make known to you all that the Father makes known to me—the inner life of the Trinity. It is only a friend who shares his most intimate experiences, the plans and hopes that flow from his shared love" (*Called: New Thinking on Christian Vocation*, p. 6). We are friends of the Lord, not mere servants. The work we do is thus a gift and a blessing, a sharing in the work of Christ. He tells us that he has revealed everything to us and chosen us. We may never come to know this unless we look at him and at our lives with an ever-deepening contemplative attitude. If truth has been revealed and an invitation has been given, then we have but to look attentively within, listen attentively to the Word, to discover what is already there as gift.

We have been accustomed in the Church to think of God-given vocations in terms of the options of priesthood, religious life, or marriage. Certainly, these are calls by God and represent great gifts to those who receive them in faith. But they do not exhaust the richness of God's calling in people's lives. It becomes clear in the documents of the Second Vatican Council that God's call reaches into the life of every person. The *Dogmatic Constitution on the Church* expresses this beautifully, with the concept of the universal call to holiness: "It is expressed in multiple ways by those individuals who, in their walk of life, strive for the perfection of charity, and thereby help others to grow" (#39). In this journey toward perfect charity, the Council says that we are to use the strengths we have received "as a gift from Christ" (#40). For the busy DRE, all the skills we use daily—administrative, educational, diplomatic, organizational, as well as theological and spiritual—are gifts given as part of the call. The vocation of the DRE may be life-long or a temporary stage in one's career, but it is, nonetheless, God's call and deserves the dignity of being recognized as such (cf. *Sharing the Light of Faith: National Catechetical Directory for Catholics of the United States*, #206). With a sense of such dignity and the magnitude of the gift that we discover more clearly every day, we can pray with the psalmist:

> I praise you, for I am fearfully and
> wonderfully made.
>
> Wonderful are your works;
> that I know very well.
>
> —Psalm 139:14

**FOR REFLECTION:**

1. If you are working as a parish DRE, do you view this job as a vocation, a call from God? When did you know that this was the work you wanted to do? Who or what was the agent of God's call for you?

2. Of your many tasks as DRE, what do you consider to be your three most important responsibilities? What part of your job do you love the most? What do you find most difficult?

3. How do you define the task of religious education in your particular parish? What results would you need to see in order to feel that you and your coworkers have been doing a good job?

4. Using the three categories of religious education defined in this chapter (evangelizing, contemplative, and formative), evaluate your work in the parish. Which one of the three is your strong point? Where do you need to put more energy? Brainstorm one way in which you might enrich your work in its weakest area.

# 2 Ezra's Necessary Tools

**T**his chapter is about the tools of the trade. A quick look around the office of a typical parish DRE will reveal a number of them. This will be the first exercise for the development or strengthening of a contemplative attitude. What are the tools at hand in our offices that facilitate doing this job? Here is a representative list, in no particular order: books, newsprint, a bell, pictures and posters, a telephone, a card file, paper, pens and pencils, folding chairs, Bibles, textbooks, videotapes, brochures, a copy of the local diocesan directory, an appointment calendar, a computer, journals, a vase of flowers, a clock, pictures of family members, pictures of saints, one or more crosses, any number of candles, boxes of cookies, boxes of crayons, boxes of tissues, music cassettes, a potted plant, purple, green, red, and white cloth.

Each of us has a different way of relating to this collection. For some, every drawer, shelf, and file cabinet is impeccably organized. These people are the efficiency experts. Those of us who are less scrupulous about order and tidiness need the efficiency experts to help keep us from falling into chaos. Needless to say, records must be kept accurately and safely, with an awareness of the need for confidentiality. If we can do this naturally, we should give thanks for such a useful gift. Otherwise, we will be fortunate to have a secretary, assistant, or volunteer who will help keep our mountains of paperwork in order. Some of the skills of good organization can be learned, even by the messiest or most mystical of us. That is why the above list of typical tools is a subject for contemplative awareness. We need to look deeply at the things around us in the office.

## EZRA THE SCRIBE

There is an interesting passage in the Gospel of Matthew that may well be applied to the work of the religious educator: "And he said to them, 'Therefore every scribe who has been trained for the kingdom of heaven is like the master of a household who brings out of his treasure what is new and what is old'" (Matthew 13:52). A scribe in the biblical context is not merely someone who copies out manuscripts but a true student of the Law, someone whose responsibility it is to pass on faithfully the rich tradition of Jewish faith and observance. *Holman's Bible Dictionary* gives these definitions for a scribe:

> SCRIBE: Person trained in writing skills and used to record events and decisions (Jeremiah 36:26; 1 Chronicles 24:6; Esther 3:12). During the Exile in Babylon educated scribes apparently became the experts in God's written Word, copying, preserving, and teaching it.

Ezra was a scribe in this sense—an expert in teaching God's Word (Ezra 7:6). A professional group of such scribes had developed by New Testament times, most being Pharisees (Mark 2:16). They interpreted the Law, taught it to disciples, and were experts in cases where people were accused of breaking the Law of Moses (*Holman Bible Dictionary for Windows*, Parsons Technology, 1994).

We can consider Ezra the scribe as one of our predecessors in the work of religious education. The Book of Nehemiah relates a moving episode in which Ezra reads and teaches the Law to all the people assembled after the return from exile and the rebuilding of the Temple:

All the people gathered together into the square before the Water Gate. They told the scribe Ezra to bring the book of the Law of Moses, which the LORD had given to Israel. Accordingly, the priest Ezra brought the Law before the assembly, both men and women and all who could hear with understanding. This was on the first day of the seventh month. He read from it facing the square before the Water Gate from early morning until midday, in the presence of the men and the women and those who could understand; and the ears of all the people were attentive to the book of the Law. The scribe Ezra stood on a wooden platform that had been made for the purpose; and beside him stood Mattithiah, Shema, Anaiah, Uriah, Hilkiah, and Maaseiah on his right hand; and Pedaiah, Mishael, Malchijah, Hashum, Hash-baddanah, Zechariah, and Meshullam on his left hand. And Ezra opened the book in the sight of all the people, for he was standing above all the people; and when he opened it, all the people stood up. Then Ezra blessed the LORD, the great God, and all the people answered, "Amen, Amen," lifting up their hands. Then they bowed their heads and worshiped the LORD with their faces to the ground. Also Jeshua, Bani, Sherebiah, Jamin, Akkub, Shabbethai, Hodiah, Maaseiah, Kelita, Azariah, Jozabad, Hanan, Pelaiah, the Levites, helped the people to understand the Law, while the people remained in their places. So they read from the book, from the law of God, with interpretation. They gave the sense, so that the people understood the reading. And all the people went their way to eat and drink and to send portions and to make great rejoicing, because they had understood the words that were declared to them.

—Nehemiah 8:1–8, 12

This scene in the life of Israel illuminates the ministry of Ezra, priest and scribe, who is not unlike the parish DRE of today. He has his primary tool: the Book of the Law of God. His reading of the book makes clear that it is not the physical book itself, nor even the text, but the actual living Word of God proclaimed to those who listen with absorption and are transformed by it. Ezra's work is reading, that is, proclamation and interpretation. His teaching is the activity by which the people are led in worship. Their response to the Word is full of ritual gesture—they stand up, they lift up their hands, they bow their heads, they fall in adoration with their faces to the ground. Moreover, they respond, "Amen, Amen" (Nehemiah 8:6). They also weep with sorrow when they hear the Law read (because they have not followed it), but upon the urging of Ezra, Nehemiah, and the Levites who teach with them, the people cease their weeping and go to their homes to eat and drink in celebration, to share portions of their feast with those who have nothing prepared for them, and to rejoice. All this response, we read, happens "because they had understood the words that were declared to them" (Nehemiah 8:12).

Compare that description of a dynamic catechetical session with the text of the RCIA that describes "suitable" catechesis (#75), cited in the first chapter. Such catechesis is to be especially supported by celebrations of the Word. It should be liturgical. It should evoke in the catechumens "a profound sense of the mystery of salvation in which they desire to participate." It should lead them to a deeper experience of prayer, an openness to share their faith with others and to live it faithfully, and a commitment to charity. These are the primary effects of Ezra's teaching as well. The people are converted to more faithful adherence to the Law. They worship God with gesture and prayer. They celebrate their joy with feasting, and they share their bounty with the poor.

## EZRA THE CATECHIST

In terms of Ezra's catechetical methods, they are really quite simple. He reads and he explains. But there is more. He makes use of a podium, so that all the people can see him. He holds the book up high, so that all can see. His way of presiding over the catechetical session shows dignity and deliberation. He opens the book before all the people in such a way that they all rise to their feet. When he reads from it—from early morning until midday—he must read in such a way that all the people are attentive. When he interprets the book, the sense is clear so that all the people understand. Finally, he leads the assembly in such a way that their attentiveness flows naturally into worship. When the session is over, the people's lives are transformed. They grow in faith through their understanding of the Law, in hope so that their tears are changed into joy, and in charity through their kindness to those in need.

What are Ezra's tools? We can list them: an appropriate place for teaching, a convenient platform so that the teacher can be seen and heard, and a book that contains God's Word for the people. But there are more important tools. Ezra has a good support team. Nehemiah, the governor, has called him and given him the authority to teach. A significant list of assistants is given, along with an unspecified number of Levites, who reinforce the teaching of Ezra and help the people to understand what he has presented. We might imagine that they go out among the crowd to answer questions and clarify for individuals what has been read. In a real sense, Nehemiah for the modern DRE is the local bishop, represented by the pastor, who has engaged him or her for the ministry of teaching and who, ideally, is standing by with the support of authority for the teaching that happens in the parish. The assistants and Levites suggest to us other members of the staff in religious education, or the parish pastoral team in general, as well as all the volunteers who give of their time and energy to work with us in catechetical ministry.

Finally, the most important tools at Ezra's disposal are ones that cannot be seen but without which no teaching is possible, even with the finest of libraries and technical resources. Ezra's principal tool is his own person and the persons of his listeners. He has a voice and a physical presence that he can rely on. But most importantly, he draws on his own store of faith and on the goodness of heart of his listeners. We must never underestimate the great power of our own desire to teach the faith we profess, or the desire of students to learn about God. What Ezra transmits to the people is not merely the content of the Book of the Law but something of his own relationship with God in terms of faith, worship, and service to God's people. This is a core meaning of tradition. The Church does not simply pass on information. It transmits the living and lived faith. The good DRE does the same.

Some other aspects of the DRE, those intangible qualities that are primary tools of the trade for us, are suggested by the list at the head of this chapter. There are included pictures, a bell, cloths in the colors of the different liturgical seasons, cassette and videotapes, candles, a vase of flowers, and images of the saints and members of one's own family. All of these things speak to the senses and therefore stimulate the imagination and the memory.

The work of religious education is not only addressed to the reasoning mind. It is a work of memory and imagination as well.

## REMEMBERING FAITHFULLY

At a critical moment in his ministry, when Jesus was almost ready to end his work as a teacher, he demonstrated one last great lesson with the injunction to do what he was doing in remembrance of him. Since then, Christians have celebrated the Eucharist, the Supper of the Lord, as the central act of worship but not of worship alone. At the heart of each celebration of the Eucharist is the *anamnesis*, the remembering of the words with which we experience again and again the risen Christ present among us. So important is this remembering that it is thought to be the principal impetus for the writing down of the Gospels, and most specifically, the passion narrative of the earliest Gospel, that of Mark. The proximate use of the story was neither evangelization nor catechesis but the need at the heart of the community gathering for worship to remember faithfully that which must be told when we share Christ's gift of himself in the shared meal of bread and wine.

As with the pictures of family, images of the Lord and of the saints are powerful reminders for adults and children about our family of faith. A vase of flowers touches the room with beauty. Candles remind us of the One who is light for the world. Liturgical colors bring hearts into harmony with the seasons of the Church's year, the mysteries of incarnation and redemption. Movies and music speak to the spirit through the senses. The work of Ezra— and the ministry of the DRE—is not merely the imparting of conceptual knowledge but the imparting of knowledge that is loving faithfulness. Therefore, the imagination and the memory are the loci for much of what we do.

That which speaks to the senses touches the heart and moves the will. For this reason our worship is based on ritual action. We use story, song, beautiful art, bodily gestures that express the inexpressible—our relationship with God. Ezra's "lesson" looks very much like a liturgical action to us. He proclaims the Word and interprets the Word. He leads the people in prayer and praise. Their hearts are filled with joy, which they celebrate with food and drink, and which they share with the poor. Our teaching, our administration, our encounters with all sorts of people will be enlivened if they are also addressed to imagination and memory as well as to the reasoning mind.

In our typical DRE's office are also such things as pens and pencils, a card file, a computer, a telephone, and similar practical objects. We may not think of them as particularly religious, but we may come to value them as sacred. They are the avenues and doorways of communication. We need to be able to be in touch with the people we serve. We need to communicate about schedules, classes, workshops, cancellations, and opportunities in a timely and efficient fashion. Not to do so would only bring confusion to our lives, and it would reflect a lack of respect for those we serve or with whom we work. Appointment books and meeting schedules may often seem like hard taskmasters of whom we are the slaves.

In most parishes, the constituency is large and the variety of tasks ever widening. To learn and use an efficient system may be daunting at first, especially for those of us who are administratively challenged, but ultimately it will be liberating. In fact, those who are not well organized by nature can benefit most from developing good habits of work and communication. Few of us have the luxury of a personal secretary who will answer correspondence, keep schedules, and remind us of appointments. No one will want to hear our message if we have kept them waiting.

The sacred objects on our desk can be effectively used to aid us in our service of the Good News.

## TIME

One of the most important items on the DRE's desk is a clock. Time is a gift. Many of us have a tendency to think we do not have enough of this gift. Some of us even claim we have no time at all. We prove this by pointing to the calendar or day planner and showing how every hour of every day of our week is fully booked with appointments, meetings, and responsibilities. No one is likely to admit that there are gaping blocks of unassigned time available in their schedules. None of us is able to change the allotment of time we are given—in a day or in a lifetime. And yet our perception of how quickly time passes and how much we can accomplish in a given amount of time varies enormously.

It does not advance our ministry when we run around in a panic about the short supply of time available to us. Hurrying is a symptom of our culture, it seems, but we do not create any extra time for ourselves by doing so. We need to be at peace with the time we do have. There are some very effective exercises for accomplishing this. Most obvious is good scheduling. Good scheduling is being accurate and conscientious about recording appointments, but it is also much more. It means being able to say "no." There are some things to which we cannot say "no": all the non-negotiables of our job. But there are also many "negotiable" things, some of which we need to let go. We cannot do everything. That is why there are other people around us.

There are also things we tend to neglect that we must include in our schedule. These include exercise, prayer, recreation, truly human conversations with friends and colleagues, meals taken in serenity, laughter, continuing education, retreats and other forms of nurture for our spiritual life, and vacations. These are the things that keep us human, that bathe our spirits in grace, that refresh body and mind, that give us new energy and hope. In a word, these are the things that fuel us for the many tasks and responsibilities on our calendars. Rather than taking away from our valuable time to "get things done," they enable us to work well and quickly. Without these things, we lose our creativity and our love for our work. We become slaves to the clock and forget that Jesus said we are his friends, not his servants.

So, one may ask, how can I schedule 20 minutes of prayer or any other pleasant thing when the job I am doing will take the next six hours, and I only have three available? The answer is simple: just stop. Some time ago, on retreat at a Benedictine monastery, I noticed that the monks and the nuns lived by a schedule. For instance, an hour might be allotted for house and garden chores in the morning. Then Mass was followed by breakfast, followed by study, followed by prayer, followed by whatever, throughout the day. There was a pace, a rhythm, where time was given to a great variety of things. When it was time to move to the next assigned activity, the members of the community simply stopped what they were doing and moved to that next thing. It was a little like a dance. The music continued, the dancing continued, but one changed partners, locations on the dance floor, and steps. Eventually one would come around to the original partner or position or step—and do that again. And so they could leave the chore, the study, the conversation, and even the prayer. They knew that those activities would be awaiting their return later or on the next day.

This seemed a very peaceful way to live out one's daily schedule. But how could anyone live that way in our busy secular world, especially working in our busy modern parishes? We are not monastics, and we cannot take refuge in the peaceful rhythm of the monastery. We may feel that our time is not our own. Things take longer than we planned. People interrupt us or they ask for more of our time than we had originally allotted for them. That is true, but it does not mean that we need to panic. We have a choice. We can politely end an activity: "I'm sorry, but we will have to continue this discussion at another time." We can tell ourselves: "This class preparation is not yet complete; I will give it more attention later." The world and the parish will certainly not come to an end if we do this. We may, in fact, find it very liberating.

It may be helpful here to examine the attitudes that affect our experience of time, especially our experience that we do not have enough time. Often what lies beneath this sense of urgency is a strong need to finish things. We do not think in terms of an allotment of time during which we can work at doing something. Rather we think in terms of getting something done and how much time that is going to take. We are focused on completing the task. That is the goal. While there is nothing wrong with wanting to complete things, it may be more useful to focus on the actual doing of the thing and allow ourselves to be pleasantly surprised when, lo and behold, it is finished.

What this means is that we focus not on the accomplishment of a task but on the work itself. It also means that we focus not on the future (completion) but on the present (the thing itself). I do not write a book. I write a sentence, or sometimes just a word or phrase. At the end there is a book—or a course of study, a project, a cake, a liturgical celebration, or a clean closet. All of these only come into being as a result of many individual moments in which we have been doing something, whether that something was standing in front of a copy machine, sifting flour, or dusting shelves. In a real sense, I cannot make a cake. I can only sift flour, measure milk, break eggs, and stir batter. As DREs, we calmly do, one at a time, all the things that are part of cake-making. In the end, we may rejoice in the delicious cake, but it is best to think of the cake itself as God's gift. We do not need to worry about it.

## TISSUES

The last tool in the office to be mentioned here is the box of tissues. Inevitably, this will be needed for someone's tears. In our role as part of the parish pastoral team, we sometimes are witnesses to the sorrows and troubles of people's lives. Our words have the power to comfort and heal. This is part of the ministry of Jesus. Sadly, our words also have the power to hurt, even to bring someone to tears. We must be on guard that our attention to tasks does not needlessly cause pain or misunderstanding. The presence of a box of tissues is a reminder to pay attention. We will learn to listen and to notice the needs and concerns of those whom we serve. The *Pastoral Constitution on the Church in the Modern World* begins with a statement about human community:

> The joys and the hopes, the griefs and the anxieties of the [people] of this age, especially those who are poor or in any way afflicted, these too are the joys and hopes, the griefs and anxieties of the followers of Christ. Indeed nothing genuinely human fails to raise an echo in their hearts (#1).

The box of tissues is a symbol of our common humanity, a reminder that ours is a ministry of the heart as well as of the mind. The box of tissues is a physical expression of our compassion.

**FOR REFLECTION:**

1. Look around your office and at your desk. Make a list of some of the things you see, your tools of the trade. Are some of these things superfluous, no longer useful, or out of date? What do you think is the most important object in your office? What would you like to remove?

2. Consider your personal gifts and abilities. Make a list of all your good qualities that help you do your work. Do you always call on your real strengths when needed? Write a prayer of thanksgiving for the natural gifts God has given you.

3. Consider any weaknesses or limitations you may have. What can you learn from this list? What impact do these disabilities have on your work? How can you use resources and your coworkers more effectively to complement your own gifts and limitations? How are you growing ministerially?

# 3 No DRE Is an Island

Knowing where to turn for help is invaluable
knowledge for a busy DRE. It is possible to feel
overwhelmed by the volume of work, but we need
to know that we are surrounded by a gifted community
that shares our mission. We saw that Ezra had the support
of the governor, Nehemiah, as well as the help of a variety
of assistants. He also had the cooperation of the Levites,
who might correspond in our case with the administrative
staff. In a modern parish of even a small size, there are
often a number of colleagues for the DRE. These might
include the pastor and associate priests, permanent
deacons, music and liturgical ministers, school personnel,
the youth minister, a director for the catechumenate or
adult education, and full- or part-time staff members for a
variety of pastoral needs, such as ministry to the bereaved,
care of the sick, spiritual direction and development, and
a coordinator for social justice and charitable outreach
ministries.

If the DRE can think of these colleagues as allies rather
than rivals, much will be gained for the good of the parish.
The staff may be seen as an alliance based on collegiality
and a shared sense of mission. However, a number of
things can militate against the development of such an
alliance. These might include an isolationist approach to
one's work (see the booklet in this series entitled *Forming
Ministerial Relationships*), a fearful territoriality that defines
too sharply the divisions between departments and persons,

the lack of a common vision of Church, the failure to discuss one's vision of Church, differences caused by strong, clashing personalities, and the fear of becoming dispensable.

## INDISPENSABLE?

Perhaps the fear of becoming dispensable is the most striking, because it so well reflects an assumption of our culture that is, in fact, not essentially Christian. In their book *Leadership in a Successful Parish*, Thomas Sweetser, S.J., and Carol Wisniewski Holden make an astonishing statement: "Staff members need to work themselves out of jobs rather than make themselves indispensable" (p. 54). The idea is that the parish staff is not what defines the local church community, the people are. A good staff empowers parishioners to take responsibility for the life and ministry of their community. That is not to say that staff members must look forward to unemployment. On the contrary, the more they are successful in facilitating the ministry of all the baptized, the more the parish will grow, in numbers and in life. The staff will have more work to do, not less.

Perhaps because the DRE is often the "jack-of-all-trades" around the parish, there is a danger of thinking we can and must do everything. In fact, it is very helpful to think of oneself as part of a team. Learning to collaborate is a very important skill.

To use a common example, the parish celebration of first Eucharist requires the input and expertise of a number of staff members, as well as volunteers. The pastor and other priests are centrally involved, as are eucharistic ministers, music and liturgy directors, people who are responsible for flowers and environment, providers of hospitality, and all who are involved in formal educational programs for the children and their parents. One way to look at the role of the DRE in this process is as a midwife to the ever-new birth of faith in people's lives. Part of this ministry involves the provision of formal educational programs. Part may be administration, or the choreography of an elaborate ballet. But all of it does tend in the direction of working ourselves out of a job, as Sweetser and Holden boldly suggest.

The work of preparing children in the ways of the faith is primarily the privilege of parents. The proper role of religious educators is to support the parents in this primary responsibility by providing catechetical programs for the children and, more importantly, for the parents, by means of opportunities for their ongoing faith formation as adults, and especially through programs that help them in their catechetical role with their children (*Sharing the Light of Faith: National Catechetical Directory for Catholics of the United States*, #212). The *Decree on the Apostolate of the Laity* of the Second Vatican Council expresses beautifully the role and dignity of parents in the religious education of their children:

> Christian husbands and wives are cooperators in grace and witnesses of faith on behalf of each other, their children, and all others in their household. They are the first to communicate the faith to their children and to educate them; by word and example they train their offspring for the Christian and apostolic life. They prudently help them in the choice of their vocation and carefully promote any religious calling which they may discern in them (#11).

It is clear from this passage that the catechetical work of the parent does not cease when the child is old enough to attend school but continues throughout their formative years. It is important for a DRE whose constituency may include a large number of children and youth to recognize that he or she is a resource for and a collaborator with all those parents.

It diminishes neither the authority nor the responsibility of the DRE to understand the religious education of children in this way. It does call attention to the communal dimension of the Church's ministry. And it stresses the centrality of the Gospel in our ministry. Our function is not to maintain adherence to the principles of our programs, however well-conceived and implemented. It is to help the people of God to grow in faith, to testify to that faith, to enter into a deeper relationship with Christ, and to live that relationship. This requires from us more creativity, openness to change, and a willingness to step aside at times. It is, however, liberating, and it will challenge us to grow in faith as well.

## COLLABORATION

Our ministry works best when we collaborate. We may take this for granted in terms of other members of the parish staff, but the circle of collaboration is much wider. It includes the entire family of faith. Every person who becomes the subject of any of the ministries of the DRE is not an object of that ministry but a partner in it, a fellow servant of the mission of the Church. St. Paul was at pains to make this point to the community at Corinth:

> Now you are the Body of Christ and individually members of it. And God has appointed in the Church first apostles, second prophets, third teachers; then deeds of power, then gifts of healing, forms of assistance, forms of leadership, various kinds of tongues. Are all apostles? Are all prophets? Are all teachers? Do all work miracles? Do all possess gifts of healing? Do all speak in tongues? Do all interpret?
> —1 Corinthians 12:27–30

We may sometimes feel like a jack-of-all-trades, but Paul reassures us that we do not need to be. There are apostles, prophets, teachers, healers, leaders, and even miracle workers all around us. Part of our job may prove to be the discovery of the gifted Body of Christ in our local communities. In our role as midwife, we may help to give birth and nurture someone else's gift. St. Paul would be content with that, for he asserts: "If one member is honored, all rejoice together with it" (1 Corinthians 12:26). Let us rejoice then.

The work of the DRE in the parish takes place in cooperation with and in conversation with many other individuals. So too the expertise, competence, and professional development of the DRE is refined by a variety of educational and ministerial contacts and resources. It is assumed that one would not have been hired for this position in the first place without appropriate theological and pastoral training. If that is not the case, it is urgent that the missing components be supplied as quickly as possible. Most dioceses have some opportunities for ministerial training. Beyond that, there are schools of theology and universities, both Catholic and secular, that offer a wide range of educational opportunities ranging from Scripture to pastoral counseling, teaching methods, conflict resolution, and group dynamics.

Even if one's basic preparation for ministry is excellent, there is always the need for continuing education and ongoing professional development. Theology is not static. There is a continuing dialogue among theologians. The parish DRE may not need to refer to this on a daily basis but should not be completely ignorant of it. At the heart of continuing education should be a special attention to Scripture study. The Gospel is the center of our work. We can never finish our own reflection on it. If our intellectual and spiritual conversation with the Scriptures is not fresh and lively, our teaching cannot possibly be so. The reality of religious education in the parish is often heavily weighted on the side of administration and maintenance of programs. We need to bring to this work the excitement of a stimulated mind and a heart dedicated to the Church's mission.

The DRE receives professional sustenance from contact with his or her counterparts in other parishes, around the diocese, and around the country. Workshops and conferences bring us into contact with ideas and procedures that may be new to us. These may challenge us to develop our programs more extensively. But most especially it is the people like us who are enmeshed in the daily work of parish life who will inspire and refresh us. With them we can freely share struggles and successes, receive suggestions and support, and return to the parish routine with a renewed energy for sharing the Good News.

## HOBNOBBING WITH WIZARDS

Toward the end of the old movie *The Wizard of Oz*, the wizard is leaving Oz in a hot air balloon to return to his home in Kansas. He tells the people of Oz that he is going to a wizards' convention "to hobnob" with his fellow wizards. This hobnobbing is necessary for us, too. In our diocese, we have periodic meetings of parish DREs. I tell people that I am going to hobnob with my fellow wizards. The meetings, of course, always have an agenda, some topics of interest to us in our work, but it is really the chance to be with my fellow DREs that gives my spirit a boost and reminds me of what this work is about. If I have been moving in an ever-so-slightly idiosyncratic direction, this diocesan connection puts me back in touch with the larger, but still local, Church.

In many areas, statewide or regional networking with other DREs is also made available through DRE associations that have formed through the efforts of peers in service to one another. Networking on this level also offers support and encouragement and at the same time contributes to broadening our perspective as well as the resources available to us. The same is true of the opportunities that exist for membership in national associations dedicated to serving the needs of DREs: the National Conference for Catechetical Leadership (NCCL) and the National Association of Parish Coordinators and Directors of Religious Education (NPCD). Information about membership in diocesan, regional, state, and national associations for DREs is available from your diocesan office.

We also need to remain connected with the universal Church as well. For most of us this happens through reading. We need to know what the pope has been saying and also what our own bishops have been discussing at their annual meeting every November in Washington. We need to know what juridical and political events have attracted their attention and comment, and what stances they have been taking in areas of social justice and human rights.

It goes without saying that all our libraries should contain copies of the documents of Vatican II, the renewed liturgical rites, the new *Code of Canon Law* (1983), the Lectionary, the RCIA, and the *Catechism of the Catholic Church*. We should take these books off the shelves from time to time, not just to look up a necessary snippet of information but simply to read for a while in one or the other. This practice will keep us in tune with the teaching Church. Finally, it is very worthwhile to subscribe to a service like the NCCB *Origins*, a weekly publication that prints the texts of papal documents and speeches, Vatican decrees, most major writings and addresses of the bishops of the United States, and other documents relevant to Catholics in the United States.

## COMMUNICATION WITH COLLEAGUES

Besides the specifically educational opportunities available to the religious educator, there are also occasions for professional development in other important areas. Not all of us are born with finely honed communication skills. We need to develop these. Such development requires not only practice but also reflective examination and sometimes even intervention. When an exchange among colleagues, for instance, has not been wholly successful, then each has an obligation to spend some time considering the missed communication. Some well placed questions can be helpful: How was I feeling during the exchange? Did we allow enough time to accomplish what we needed to do? Were there other persons or situations interfering with the exchange? When I was speaking, what was the goal of my communication—really? Did I listen carefully? What did I expect to hear? Was this affecting what I really did hear?

Ideally, colleagues should then be able to share the fruits of this reflection with one another. It is always less threatening—and more truthful—to discuss difficult situations by means of "I statements": I felt confused after our meeting, I am troubled by what I think you meant, I am not sure I understand all the implications of this situation or decision, and so on. Obviously, it is important to develop careful ways of listening. The other person deserves our attention as much as we wish to receive his or hers. Really listening is a great gift we can give to one another. To have one's statements listened to and truly received is an affirmation of our dignity. When one listens with full attention, one must set aside one's own agenda. This is not the time to be thinking of one's next response, or of what will happen later, or of what has been upsetting in the past. The person who really listens actually dies to self, for he or she chooses to make another the whole focus of attention. (For a more detailed treatment of

communication, see the booklet in this series entitled
*Communicating Effectively*.)

We do not live in an ideal world, however, and it would
be naive to think that Church membership or employment
somehow confers perfection. In fact, the contrary is true.
We notice even more our own and others' imperfection,
because we expect that we and they will be better than the
rest of the world since we are followers of Jesus. We are
not better, but we have a conscious intention to grow in
charity and justice. When we fail, the discrepancy between
our lives and the faith we proclaim is all the more evident.

This being the case, it is sometimes necessary for staff
members and working groups to enlist the aid of a professional facilitator, someone outside the immediate parish
situation and trained in group dynamics and listening
skills. This person can help us to begin the conversation
described in the previous paragraph, can calm us down,
and can help us to remain focused on the matter at hand.
The ideal facilitator is both a coach and a referee. He or
she can help us avoid personal attacks, while still being
able to confront our differences in an authentic and con-
structive way. The facilitator is an ally for the team, a
friend to each of the partners in dialogue, and the person
able to maintain an unbiased attitude about the issues
under discussion.

As pastoral leaders in busy parishes, DREs should be
able to discern when the help of an outside facilitator is
called for but should also learn the basic skills necessary to
mediate conflict when it arises among coworkers and volunteers. Sometimes a professional intervention is not necessary, but what is needed is someone who will call the
group to reflect on the process by which it works and
communicates. If we discover ways to listen well and to be
sensitive to our own rising emotions, they will not be able
to carry us away. Then we can help others do the same.

This is an important part of good leadership. The DRE is often in a position to relate professionally to every other member of the parish staff, simply because the ministry of religious education is so broad and diversified. This provides an opportunity to build bridges of understanding and reconciliation. The work environment will be more pleasant, and all will be able to minister more effectively toward building up the Body of Christ.

## FOR REFLECTION:

1. Make a list of the people on your parish staff. Consider each of them, one by one. How do you relate to each of these people professionally? Which ones do you know best? Which would you like to know better? Are there areas of friction with one or another that you would like to improve? Think of one action that might help this situation.

2. Do you know the various people who minister in your local diocesan office? Do you make use of the resources of your diocese to enrich your catechetical ministry? Take time to learn about one diocesan office that you do not know well.

3. How well do you listen to colleagues and parishioners? Do people find you accessible? Do you feel adequately listened to by your coworkers? What happens at your parish when there are conflicts among staff members? How do you respond to conflict and confrontation? What practices might you use to improve communication?

# 4   Can the DRE Have a Life?

In the second chapter, it was suggested that the most important tool we have in our ministry is our self, the person we are. Like all tools, we need maintenance. But we are more than mere tools for the work we do. We are people. Like all people, we have strengths and weaknesses, joys and sorrows, good times and hard times. We often disregard these personal dimensions for the sake of our work and for the sake of others. If we are parents or members of a religious community, we are even more aware of the need to set our own concerns aside for the sake of the family or the community. This is a good habit to have formed, but it is not the only habit we need to learn. We are not merely servants of the community. Jesus calls us not servants any longer but friends (John 15:15). We are part of the community. We are one of the family. As such, like any other member, we have needs and rights.

There is a danger that people in the helping professions can think they can always be available. Educators fall into this category and into this danger as well. It is related to the attitude that we are indispensable. If we move toward the attitude that we want to work ourselves out of a job, then we may find our newfound dispensability quite liberating. If we do not do this, we face the possibility of burnout. This is not just a bit of pastoral or psychological jargon but a real crisis for the one who experiences it. There are warning signs: tiredness even at the beginning of a day, irritability, a sense of urgency or that there is never enough time, inability to concentrate or complete tasks, anxiety, and a decrease of passion, joy, and enthusiasm for one's work. John Sanford's book, *Ministry Burnout*, is very informative about the diagnosis and treatment for this particular malaise.

## WORK OR LIFE?

It is important that we not confuse our work with our lives. A good question to ask from time to time is: If I left my job, or even if I were discharged from my job, would I still be myself? If I were incapacitated, would the parish come to a grinding halt or, worse, degenerate into chaos? Of course, one might have a financial crisis or a health-related emergency. Certainly we would mourn the loss of a position that brought a sense of purpose and satisfaction, as well as the experience of participating in the Church's mission of witnessing to the Gospel. But one should not be experiencing a loss of identity.

The best way to avoid such burnout is to know ourselves well. We need to have an understanding of our own personalities. What are the strengths and weaknesses, gifts and limitations, that are so much a part of who we are, that we might not even notice them? How do we come to notice them then? The simplest way is that those who love us will tell us. We need to have intimate and ongoing human friendships. For most people, family is the primary locus for such relationships. Most are married, and usually spouses grow over the years into a deep and loving friendship. When we can tell our stories and share our fears and hopes with one another, then we reveal ourselves and see ourselves revealed in this intimate exchange. But even if not married, everyone has a family of origin in whose midst we have already learned much about ourselves. Families need not be perfect for this grace to be experienced by their members.

Whatever the family structure may have been, all of us have the opportunity to develop and nurture good friendships during our lives. This is not coincidental to our ministry in the Church. It is at the heart of it. The God who is revealed to us by Jesus, whom we name Trinity, is by nature a relational God. It is of the essence of God to give and receive love. In fact, "God is love" (1 John 4:8). If, as we believe, we are created in the likeness of God, then being in loving relationships is of the essence of being human. The constant refrain of that First Letter of John is the mutual love at the heart of Christian life and community. For those of us in formal service to that community, our loving friends will nourish us for our hard work, comfort us in struggles and failures, rejoice with us in growth and success, and challenge us to move to new fields of mission.

There may be times, however, when the companionship of friends is not sufficient for our mental health. Then we need to know where to turn for professional assistance. There are support groups for people in ministry and for people confronting all sorts of personal challenges: bereavement, marital or family stress, substance abuse, and every sort of illness or disability. We sometimes specifically need the presence of others who share our particular burden. This kind of support can be very healing. In addition, we may avail ourselves of the services of counselors, therapists, and various kinds of doctors.

The Gospel of Mark recounts the Pharisees' criticism of Jesus for associating with disreputable people: "When Jesus heard this, he said to them, 'Those who are well have no need of a physician, but those who are sick; I have come to call not the righteous but sinners'" (Mark 2:17). It is good to know that Jesus expects us to come to him out of our need, which may be physical, emotional, or spiritual. It is not necessary to have our lives and affairs in order before we can be his friends and coworkers. We do, however, need to recognize our dysfunction and be willing to seek help. If we cannot do this, then our disabilities will inhibit our ministry. If we deny their presence, they will surface in ways that are destructive to collegiality and to the work we do. If we acknowledge them and give them conscious attention, then they will become a source of grace in our ministry.

The late Henri Nouwen's *The Wounded Healer* (1972), which has become a classic for ministers, illuminates the theme of our weakness as the place where God is strong. Nouwen tells the Talmudic story of a man who sits by the village gate. He unbinds and binds up his wounds, but not all at once. Rather, he unbinds and binds up just one wound at a time, so that he might be able to jump up to help someone else should the need arise. For the Christian, of course, the model of the wounded healer is Jesus. Nouwen writes:

> Jesus has given this story a new fullness by making his own broken body the way to health, to liberation and new life. Thus like Jesus, he who proclaims liberation is called not only to care for his own wounds and the wounds of others but also to make his wounds into a major source of his healing power. (pp. 82–83)

There is no questioning the fact of our woundedness. That is a given of human life. None of us escapes the reality of grief, failure, and illness. The only question is: How shall we live and minister, given the nature of our specific wounds? Religious education leadership in the parish will be most effective when we become conscious of our own brokenness, but not as cause for discouragement, an excuse for inaction, or an all-absorbing preoccupation. Rather, it will be for us an awareness of our commonality

with all of humanity, especially with those around us in the
community of faith. From this experience of commonality
will grow insight, compassion, and healing. We will have
insight into the needs of others as well as into our own
need for grace. We will have compassion and patience
with our own slowness and imperfection, as well as that of
others. And in working out of our woundedness, for the
good of all, we too will find healing for our wounds.

## TASK DELIVERY SYSTEM?

An important consideration in the management of work
and the time available is the question of priorities. Not all
tasks are equally important. Tasks are not necessarily the
most important portions of the day. We know all the
things we must do, so much so that sometimes we forget
the importance of simply being. If tasks were the only
consideration, our jobs could eventually be performed
by computers and robots. The Church could develop a
delivery system for religious education that might be
like banking with an ATM machine. The first thing that
people need when they come through our office door
is a person.

On our best days, people see a person who is rested,
healthy, and recollected. Good questions to ask are: Am I
well rested? Have I allotted time today for exercise? meals
taken away from my desk? prayer? quiet reflection? The
pleasant company of family and friends? Whoever does
not have time for these things cannot be really present to
the parish. We are not functionaries, still less machines.
We have bodies, emotions, and a spiritual life. Taking
care of these will not slow down our ministry but give it
integrity and energy. We will remain grounded physically,
emotionally, and spiritually, that is, in touch with the
Earth, in relationship with the other creatures—human

and nonhuman—who walk this planet, and we will be attentive to the voice of God leading and guiding us.

Jesus knew the value of time spent away from his work. The Gospels are filled with notices that he set a high priority on time spent alone, in prayer, in the life-giving company of a few friends, and even partying. These activities do not detract from his ministry. Rather, they are fuel for it. In fact, the story of Jesus' first miracle, and hence the beginning of his public ministry, takes place at a wedding reception, according to John's Gospel. Jesus is there, along with his mother and his disciples, simply as a guest at the wedding. We can assume that the bride or groom, or both, is a close friend or relative of Jesus. When his mother points out the shortage of wine, he seems unconcerned: "Woman, what concern is that to you and to me? My hour has not yet come" (John 2:4).

Interestingly, it is the mother of Jesus who pushes him to do something for the bridal couple by directing the servants to do whatever he should tell them. Family and friends who form part of our private life often have the power to profoundly influence our public life. Like the mother of Jesus, they have the insight to see what we can really do. They see our possibilities. Then they point out that potential to us. They reveal who we are and who we are becoming.

The Cana story is especially significant for us because it illustrates something that often happens in the course of our attempts to follow the call of God in our lives. The ministry of Jesus begins because of what seems to be an inconvenience and a disruption. The party, which represents the expected course of events, is in fact interrupted. What we expect is not necessarily what is most important at any given moment. What we expect is not our life. Our life is what really happens, and that reality is often quite a surprise, not at all what we had planned, an interruption to our way of thinking. God's way of living calls us to pay attention to the details, the interruptions, the family and friends along the way. Such attentiveness is refreshing, and it leads us into our service of the community, not away from it.

## PAUL'S BOAST

When we read the letters of St. Paul, that tireless apostle still appears very human and very vulnerable, with his personality very much visible in his ministry. In a moment of extraordinary self-revelation, he writes to the Corinthians of his great graces as well as his struggles and genuine weakness, and his frustration with that weakness:

> If I must boast, I will boast of the things that show my weakness. The God and Father of the Lord Jesus (blessed be he forever!) knows that I do not lie. In Damascus, the governor under King Aretas guarded the city of Damascus in order to seize me, but I was let down in a basket through a window in the wall, and escaped from his hands.
>
> It is necessary to boast; nothing is to be gained by it, but I will go on to visions and revelations of the Lord. I know a person in Christ who 14 years ago was caught up to the third heaven—whether in the body or out of the body I do not know; God knows. And I know that such a person—whether in the body or out of the body I do not know; God knows—was caught up into paradise and heard things that are not to be told, that no mortal is permitted to repeat. On behalf of such a one I will boast, but on my own behalf I will not boast, except of my weaknesses. But if I wish to boast, I will not be a fool, for I will be speaking the truth. But I refrain from it, so that

no one may think better of me than what is seen in me or heard from me, even considering the exceptional character of the revelations. Therefore, to keep me from being too elated, a thorn was given me in the flesh, a messenger of Satan to torment me, to keep me from being too elated. Three times I appealed to the Lord about this, that it would leave me, but he said to me, "My grace is sufficient for you, for power is made perfect in weakness." So, I will boast all the more gladly of my weaknesses, so that the power of Christ may dwell in me. Therefore I am content with weaknesses, insults, hardships, persecutions, and calamities for the sake of Christ; for whenever I am weak, then I am strong.

—2 Corinthians 11:30—12:10

What this passage reveals to us is the great self-awareness of St. Paul. He knows his history and can recite it with relish. Obviously he takes some pride in his adventures, especially the escape in a basket. He knows the rich graces and blessings he has received and writes of the extraordinary revelations and mystical experience that God has given him. At first he almost shyly uses the third person— "I know a person in Christ," but it quickly becomes clear that he is talking about himself: "But I refrain from it, so that no one may think better of me than what is seen in me or heard from me, even considering the exceptional character of the revelations. Therefore, to keep me from being too elated, a thorn was given me in the flesh, a messenger of Satan to torment me, to keep me from being too elated" (12:6-7). The gift of God causes him great elation, and he cannot keep from sharing it and yet does not want anyone to give him the credit for this gift.

Paul knows the danger of losing touch with his limitations in the consciousness of God's presence. And so he also acknowledges the weakness that has plagued him. There have been numerous opinions about the nature of Paul's thorn in the flesh. Was it a physical ailment? Everything—from blindness to psoriasis, to his short stature, to epilepsy—has been suggested. Or it may have even been some sort of temptation to sin, to doubt, or even a desire to leave his ministry for the sake of marriage and family life.

Perhaps it is well for us that we do not know what this weakness of Paul's was. What is important is that we become acquainted with our own thorns in the flesh, whether they are physical or mental disabilities, emotional shortcomings, temptations to sin, or actual sins. Like St. Paul, we will then learn that it is only in our weaknesses and limitations that we discover the power of God working within us. Unlike Paul, we may find it difficult to be "content with weaknesses, insults, hardships, persecutions, and calamities for the sake of Christ" (12:10). Most of us try to avoid at least the calamities. Nevertheless, it may be helpful to remember from time to time that persecution and hardship is what Jesus experienced and said would be normative for his followers. It can be liberating to discover that we are not responsible for the success of our mission, only the effort. God will take care of the harvest. That is what St. Paul experienced, and there has never been a more successful evangelist than he.

## FOR REFLECTION:

1. What are the persons, places, and activities that refresh and renew you? Do you spend enough time on the things that give you energy and enthusiasm? Where do you go when you need to be alone? Do you notice a difference in yourself when you spend time alone, in prayer, or with friends?

2. What are the weaknesses or wounds to which you must attend? Do you now experience or have you ever experienced burnout? What is that like? What resources are available to you to restore your joy and energy? What practical steps can you take to avoid losing your joy and energy at home and at work?

3. Do you feel indispensable? What would happen to the people around you if you decided to take a vacation, go on a retreat, or temporarily postpone some of your work? Do the people you work with experience you as a person with a life outside the parish setting? Do you? If you lost your job tomorrow, what would you do? How would you feel?

# 5 Loaves and Fishes for the Spirit

The story of the multiplication of the loaves and fishes, told six times in the Gospels, has something to say to busy DREs. The apostles, who had been working all day with Jesus, assisting, teaching, and healing, are frustrated and suggest sending all the people away. The people are too many, and the resources are too few. The apostles are convinced that they have nothing left to give: "When it grew late, his disciples came to him and said, 'This is a deserted place, and the hour is now very late; send them away so that they may go into the surrounding country and villages and buy something for themselves to eat'" (Mark 6:35).

Of course, we know that Jesus is not going to accede to this suggestion. However, unless we know the context of the story as told in the Gospel of Mark, we may be inclined to judge the apostles all too harshly. The story of the feeding of the five thousand (Mark 6:35–44) is preceded by the beginning of the evangelistic mission of the apostles themselves (6:6–13) and the story of the death of John the Baptist (6:14–29). And just before the telling of the feeding of the multitude are some preliminary remarks about the movements of Jesus and the apostles while they were out of the public eye (6:30–34). All these episodes and details need to be considered together in order to understand what happens to the apostles in terms of awareness and religious experience.

## COMMISSIONED COMPANIONS

At the beginning of chapter 6, Mark tells of the commissioning of the apostles for ministry. "He called the Twelve and began to send them out two by two, and gave them authority over the unclean spirits" (6:7). This is the text to which all Christian evangelizers and missionaries have looked over the centuries for inspiration and guidance. It provides for companionship: They are to work in teams. It gives authority to their work: They will be doing what Jesus has done. And it sets them, like him, clearly in the front lines of the battle against evil.

The text continues with guidelines for the simplicity of life that will be a mark of the followers of Jesus: "He ordered them to take nothing for their journey except a staff; no bread, no bag, no money in their belts; but to wear sandals and not to put on two tunics" (6:8–9). This material divestment signaled a freedom from anxiety, an authentic poverty of spirit, and a reliance on God's providence that has been a source of direction for countless saints and heroes in the history of the Church, most notably St. Francis of Assisi, who took it quite literally, and in our day, Mother Teresa and Dorothy Day. The many-branched Franciscan family, the Missionaries of Charity, and the Catholic Worker movement are eloquent testimony to the fertile faith of their founders, who did not hesitate to take this Gospel text literally.

Finally, this section ends with the statement that the apostles did, in fact, do all the things that Jesus did. These are summed up in three categories: They proclaimed repentance, they cast out demons, and they cured the sick. That is to say: They taught, they overcame evil when they encountered it, and they did good to people.

The next passage is the story of the martyrdom of John the Baptist. Its placement here is not coincidental. John is the model of the apostle. Jesus calls him the greatest man ever to have been born (Matthew 11:11). John is the greatest of the prophets, the summit of faithfulness in relation to all the prophets of Israel, and a model for Christians. Yet he does not escape imprisonment and a gruesome death. He stands as a link between the Hebrew and the Christian revelations, an heir of Elijah and a precursor of Jesus. He is popularly thought of in terms of an Elijah resurrected from the dead (6:15). Even Herod uses this concept: "John, whom I beheaded, has been raised" (6:16). Although John's fate, on the surface, is certainly one to be avoided, he is actually the first example of Christian hope, of faith in the resurrection. The story includes the detail of his disciples taking his body and burying it, an allusion to the entombment of Jesus as well. The story, like the paschal mystery to which it points, is a paradox, presented at this particular point to prepare us for the amazing experience of the loaves and fishes.

The prologue, as it were, to the story of the loaves and fishes takes place backstage, away from the crowds of people. The disciples, elated at their missionary success, tell Jesus everything they have done and taught since he sent them out (6:30). He suggests to them a kind of retreat: "He said to them, 'Come away to a deserted place all by yourselves and rest a while.' For many were coming and going, and they had no leisure even to eat" (6:31). The disciples need rest, relaxation, and food. They are depleted and hungry, physically, emotionally, and spiritually. And so they go to spend some time alone.

In the meantime, the crowds of people discover where Jesus and the disciples have gone and hurry after them (6:33). The presence of the crowd, also depleted and hungry, fills Jesus with compassion and is the impetus for the multiplication of the loaves and fishes. Jesus does not merely provide food for the people. This story is not about instant gratification or fast food. The tale proceeds liturgically, with the active participation of the disciples, who gather the people on the grass in orderly groups. It includes eucharistic actions, which would have been immediately recognized by early Christians reading this Gospel: Jesus took, blessed, broke, and gave bread (6:41). And the disciples are the ones called to set this meal before the people. Finally, it is made clear that there is a great abundance of food, more than is needed. There are many leftovers, 12 baskets full of broken remnants, a symbol of the broken but entire people of God.

## COMMISSIONED COMMUNITY

What has all this to do with spirituality for the DRE? Much. The DRE, like all who work to spread the Word of God, is first of all a person sent. However, none of us is sent alone. We are on this mission with companions. The fact that the disciples go out two by two is not meant to focus on two as the proper size of a mission team but rather to illustrate that one is not enough. We need to be a community when we speak the Good News. For us, that is a strength and a freedom. We have help. Our spirituality then needs a strong dimension of community and of mutual reliance, not self-reliance. Our spirituality becomes trinitarian, reflecting the very life of God.

The disciples are sent out without much in the way of material support. We are usually given many more resources to accomplish our tasks. But as Jesus says to Martha about her sister Mary, "Martha, Martha, you are worried and distracted by many things; there is needed only one thing. Mary has chosen the better part, which will not be taken away from her" (Luke 10:41–42).

Sometimes it is possible to let the tasks and the details distract us from the one thing that is necessary. Mary chooses simply to sit at the feet of Jesus, listening to him.

This we must do. The spirituality of the religious educator will be fertile only if it is truly Christ-centered. We may have all the skills and methods in the world, but our ministry will be empty if we do not have Christ at the center of our lives and our work. We need to spend more time looking at him and listening to him than anything else we do in the service of the Church's mission.

Because our spirituality, like that of the disciples, is Christ-centered, it will lead us to do the things that he did: proclaim the Gospel, do good to people, and resist evil. A spirituality is not Christian if these things, in some form, are not the fruits of it. Even those called to a specifically contemplative life in enclosed monastic communities do not live out their vocations as a way of escaping from the world or as a form of self-absorption. Rather, through their life of prayer and whatever work they do, they bring the whole world with its needs and cares into their daily life. How much more so should we, who are called to an apostolic ministry in the Church, develop a spirituality that leads us out to share Good News and abundant life with others.

The disciples have before them the example of John the Baptist, who proclaimed God's Word with courage and paid the price of his life for his faithfulness to his call. John—prophet and martyr—stands at this point in Mark's Gospel as a beacon for us. Prophecy and martyrdom rarely form part of the job description for a DRE, but they are normative aspects of authentic Christian spirituality. And so our spiritual life should lead us to a growth that gives the courage to speak the truth we have learned. "Always be ready to make your defense to anyone who demands from you an accounting for the hope that is in you" (1 Peter 3:15). Finally, we will be less anxious and more at peace if we recognize that John and Jesus show us the path. We should not be surprised to find ourselves walking along it. Our spirituality, then, will include the cross, not as an expression of masochism or of passivity but as a willingness to embrace reality and to live our lives as Jesus did, with love and forgiveness.

## COME AWAY AND REST

After the missionary journey, Jesus invites the disciples: "Come away to a deserted place all by yourselves and rest a while" (Mark 6:31). We too need to pay attention to this invitation. We accept as a given, although we do not always heed it, that physical rest and sleep restore the strength of our bodies. Likewise, the spirit can become exhausted. It is fortunate that there are many places and resources available to us for spiritual retreats: retreat houses and spirituality centers of all kinds. What is important is an opportunity to be away and quiet for a while.

Our Catholic tradition includes a rich legacy of spiritual direction and various ways for being on retreat. We will choose the ones that suit our temperament and our particular stage along the journey of faith. Sometimes we will simply choose the retreat opportunities that are most convenient. It may even be that we make our retreat at home or on vacation. What is important, however, is simply that the time away gives us an opportunity to deepen our relationship with God, to grow in awareness of ourselves and of God's presence. We need quiet in which to listen to God—not necessarily physical quiet but certainly inner quiet. If our retreat helps us to do that, then it will enrich our authentic Christian spirituality.

We notice that the disciples do not have very much of a retreat. It only lasts as long as the boat trip across the lake. In fact, Mark notes that there are so many people milling around that the disciples and Jesus have not even had an opportunity to eat. This detail may sound very familiar to some DREs. All of us have days when there is no time for lunch or we eat it at our desks. The reality is that interruptions call us away from our retreat, from our quiet times, and from our efforts to nourish body and soul. We cannot drive the interruptions away. Jesus gives an example by being willing to change his agenda. His intent was to lead the disciples to a deserted place. When they arrive there, however, they find a crowd of people. Mark says, "He had compassion for them, because they were like sheep without a shepherd; and he began to teach them many things" (6:34).

The disciples do not learn the lesson immediately. As evening approaches, they want to send the hungry people away. Jesus then challenges them to do something themselves to feed the people. They think they do not even have enough resources for themselves, but he shows them that in fact there is much more than is needed. It may often seem to us like there is just no more energy for the needs of our ministry, but an appropriate spirituality for the DRE, for any Christian minister, will include a willingness to set our own plans aside, to deal with the unexpected. It will mean being ready for the interruptions, able to see in them God's presence, and to experience through them God's blessing.

The climax of the series of stories in Mark 6 is, of course, the multiplication of the loaves and fishes. This is the high point of Christian life, a model of the Eucharist. In this story we find the elements of a true eucharistic spirituality. Jesus stands at the center of the scene. It is he who feeds the people, leads the people, and blesses the people. But the disciples are an integral part of the work. They minister to the people with Jesus and in his name. Jesus gives the bread and fish, but the disciples distribute it. Through the Spirit alive in the Church, Jesus gives himself to the world, but we are his hands and his feet, his voice and his heart. We are called to bring his compassion, his bread, and his peace to one another. At the end of this story, the disciples too have been fed with enough bread and fish for their needs of the day. If we live a eucharistic life, we too shall be fed, in our times of quiet and rest, and also in our times of work and busyness.

## SPIRITUALITY

There are many legitimate spiritualities within the Catholic Christian tradition. The specific kind of spirituality one practices will often depend on various circumstances, accidents, and choices: such things as family of origin, the religious experiences of childhood, theological education and ministerial training, personality, and the details of one's life history. If we resonate to the joyful, peacemaking, and nature-loving St. Francis, our spirituality may be Franciscan. Someone whose primary experience of God comes in the deep silence of contemplative prayer may develop a Carmelite spirituality. Many teachers owe much to the contributions of the Dominicans or the Jesuits for their spiritual nurture.

There are spiritualities that emphasize our roots in Judaism, our connection with the Earth, social justice, or our relation with people of other faiths. Authentic Christian spiritualities draw from every ethnic group and cultural tradition on the face of the Earth. There are strong traditions in Catholicism of devotion to the Blessed Mother, to particular saints, and to various titles of Jesus such as the Sacred Heart. There are innumerable prayer forms, styles of meditation, sources of spiritual reading, and ascetical disciplines. There are norms for fasting, keeping vigil, and going on pilgrimage. There are retreat structures that nurture these diverse spiritual paths. Not only clergy and religious but also lay people today have access to every opportunity for spiritual growth: from the spiritual exercises of St. Ignatius, to silent contemplative retreats, to small faith-sharing groups, to Cursillo. All of these and more have a rightful place in Catholic spirituality.

It is important for us to discern which of the vast spiritual offerings available to us, and to the people with and for whom we minister, are useful and appropriate. What criteria can help sort out the abundance of opportunities at our disposal? There are some obvious standards that can be applied. First, we might return to the story of the loaves and fishes and apply what we have learned there to our own search for a spiritual path. Does the spirituality we practice support our ministry and lead us to a deeper sense of mission? Is it communal and collegial, or does it allow us to remain in our individualism? Does it help us grow in compassion and solidarity with all of God's people? Does it encourage a simple life and a spirit of poverty, or does it distract us from God and God's people by absorption in too many details and formal observances? Does it recall for us our Christian vocation as prophets and martyrs? Does it stir up in us faith, hope, and love for God and neighbor? Does it give us time to pay quiet attention to God at work in our lives? And yet does it make room for the inevitable interruptions that call us to service of one another? Is it liturgical and eucharistic? Does it hold us to more faithful living of the Gospel? Is it Christ-centered?

Finally, a useful way of coming to an appropriate spirituality for people who minister in the Church is to look at the model of the renewed catechumenate. The catechumenate is primarily about formation: the formation of faithful, lifelong Christians. That is also the challenge of every baptized person. Our formation as followers of Jesus is ongoing. We can look for direction to some of the important dimensions of catechumenal formation: It is based on Scripture, takes place in community, has as its goal a gradual and continuing conversion of life, and is celebrated liturgically. These basic principles must be present for our Christianity to be whole. There are many paths that lead this way, but all paths must begin with the Jesus we meet in the Gospels and lead us, in the company of the whole Church, into the life of the Trinity.

## FOR REFLECTION:

1. Make a list of some practices that form part of your own spiritual life. Which of these practices challenge you to reach out to others in service and fellowship? Which help you to focus more deeply on God dwelling within you? Do you spend regular time in prayer with others? Do you spend regular time praying alone? What place do the sacraments have in your life?

2. Have you made any retreats lately? What kind of retreat is most helpful to you? What kind of retreat is more challenging? Is it more difficult for you to remain silent for an extended period of time or to share your inner life with others?

3. Do your spiritual practices lead you to experience a deeper relationship with God as Trinity? Do you feel spiritually nourished or depleted most of the time? How do you use Scripture for your daily prayer? Who are the saints, canonized or not, who inspire and guide you?

# 6 For All the Saints

I t should be comforting for the beleaguered DRE to know that we do not do this job alone. Mention has already been made of the parish staff or pastoral team as a collegial association sharing a common mission. Beyond that, every DRE stands in dynamic relationship to the whole Church, past, present, and future. We profess in the Creed that we believe in the communion of saints, but we sometimes act as though we are isolated on a spiritual desert island with no contact beyond our individual constituencies. Stress arises when we cannot see our achievements or our struggles in the context of the whole mission of the Church. We know that the parish is not the whole Church, but we forget that the parish is not even really the "local Church." The local Church is the diocese. Within each parish are great numbers of domestic churches, which are, as Vatican II reminds us, the fundamental church units—Christian families (*Dogmatic Constitution on the Church*, #11, and *Decree on the Apostolate of the Laity*, #11).

It should be liberating for parish workers to recall that the parish itself is neither the first nor the greatest ecclesial unit, even if it is, nonetheless, a busy hub of activity. In the *Decree on the Apostolate of the Laity*, we read that the parish "brings together the many human differences found within its boundaries and draws them into the universality of the Church" (#10). In the day-to-day work of the parish minister, it is easy to lose sight of this universality and of the fact that our work is just a part of an enormous tapestry that only the eyes of God can take in all at once.

## LOCAL CHURCH, UNIVERSAL CHURCH

There are some practical ways to keep ourselves mindful of the Church's extension over time and around the planet. We need to develop a knowledge of the Church's history, an awareness of its presence in every form of human culture and society, and a consciousness of the eschatological dimension of its mission. These three exercises will prevent our becoming idolatrous about the Church of our own limited experience. We will catch sight of the Church's organic life and growth reaching back to the time of Jesus, spreading over the globe, being enriched by and transforming myriad cultures, and ultimately stretching forward toward the coming reign of God. We will understand that the Church gives us intimations of, but is not identical to, that promised reign.

In terms of history, we need to have a sense of the apostolic Church, the early thrust of evangelization. We share a common purpose with the apostolic age. The Church today, as then, is still sent to bring Christ to those who have not yet received him. When we recognize this, we have a corrective to the common error that says the work of the parish is the spiritual and moral nurture of the members of the parish. On the contrary, the internal nurture of the parish only serves its real work, which is to present itself as a sacrament of Christ's presence within its local community. In the *Dogmatic Constitution on the Church*, the Council Fathers wrote: "By her relationship with Christ, the Church is a kind of sacrament or sign of intimate union with God, and of the unity of all mankind. She is also an instrument for the achievement of such union and unity" (#1). The way in which this mission of the Church will be accomplished is by "proclaiming the Gospel to every creature" (#1). It should be professionally useful and personally refreshing for the DRE to be reminded of this from time to time. It may be part of our job to remind our coworkers of it as well.

A DRE with a sense of history will also be knowledge-able about the development of Church structures through-out the early centuries. Then we can understand the roots of our ministerial roles, our hierarchical order, the forma-tion of liturgical rites, sacred music, sacramental ritual, the catechumenate, the acceptance of infant baptism, and the particularly Catholic optimism about the secular world, its science, arts, and governance. If we know this history, we will easily be able to resonate with the renewal of the Second Vatican Council which, in fact, recalls us to this benevolent sense of creative partnership between the Church and the overall human endeavor.

Having a sense of Church history will open our eyes to the capacity for grave error and sinfulness within the institution, its leaders, its communities, and each of its members. But we will also be rewarded and humbled by an ever-expanding vision of the real holiness of the Church. If we learn about the lives of certain Renaissance popes, we will hardly be morally paralyzed if we discover corruption and conflict in the Church today. One of the most amazing things we encounter again and again in Scripture is the revelation that God continues to function salvifically within an arena of human sinfulness. The story told about King David in 2 Samuel 11 and 12 is a particu-larly obvious case. The adultery with Bathsheba, which most people readily recall, is hardly the most serious evil in this story. Rather, the fact that David arranges for the murder of Bathsheba's husband, Uriah, in order to cover up the adultery, can hold its own next to any of the scan-dals reported about political or religious leaders today.

It is not so surprising that God uses the saints to achieve the divine purpose. What is surprising is how God works in the midst of depravity! Nor do we only find examples in the Old Testament. We need to look no further than the apostles themselves. The Church belongs to this tradition. A sense of its humanity is very helpful in keeping us from impossible expectations of our colleagues, our pastors, our parishioners, and, of course, ourselves. At the same time, when we encounter real sanctity, wisdom, and devotion, we can be all the more likely to praise the God who does such wonders by means of earthen vessels. The fruit of this understanding will be joy and praise—gifts we need to recognize as an integral part of all authentic religious education.

If understanding the history of the Church gives us a sense of its development and continuity over time, understanding the great diversity of human culture will help us see the Church from a more global perspective. At the parish level, it may seem that the relationship of the DRE with the parish school, installing a new phone system, instituting or abolishing bingo, or setting the date of first Communion are issues of enormous urgency that can blossom into crises. However, it is a big Church, and there are many ways of accomplishing its mission. For an ethnically mixed parish in a large city, where exuberant liturgies may last two or three hours, a suburban parish's concerns about clearing out the parking lot efficiently in order to accommodate five Sunday Masses of precisely 55 minutes each will seem ludicrous. We need to come to know one another to be reminded of what is central in our faith and central to our ministry.

## A DIVERSE COMMUNITY

In the United States, there is enormous diversity within the Catholic community. And yet our education and pastoral experience have not always prepared us to think in terms of a pluralistic society and its needs. We discovered after the Second Vatican Council that the liturgy of the Church can and should speak in the languages of the world's peoples, but our theology and pedagogical methods still primarily reflect the culture of Western Europe and the experience of the immigrant Church of nineteenth-century America. The Catholic Church in America now ministers to people from every continent. A single parish may have liturgical celebrations and pastoral ministries in three or more languages. Often there will be bilingual and even trilingual priests and staff members. This pluralism within the parish requires more work and attention of us, but it enriches our experience of Church, it broadens our outlook, and it keeps us from becoming narrow-minded. We run the risk of institutionalizing the cultural specifics of our own small world and then equating that cultural institution with the Church of Christ, the correct way to worship, the only way to teach, the Gospel itself, and even the reign of God.

The Gospel of Matthew makes this point in chapter 8. Jesus has been approached by a Roman centurion who asks him to cure his sick child. When Jesus agrees to go with him, the centurion protests. Jesus need only speak a word, and the child will recover. The centurion knows his own authority and, therefore, has faith in that of Jesus. Jesus looks at him with amazement and contrasts the centurion's extraordinary faith with that of his own countrymen and co-religionists who do not acknowledge him at all. "Truly I tell you, in no one in Israel have I found such faith. I tell you, many will come from east and west and will eat with Abraham and Isaac and Jacob in the kingdom of heaven, while the heirs of the kingdom will be thrown into the outer darkness, where there will be weeping and gnashing of teeth" (Matthew 8:10–12). It is no coincidence that the first visitors to the infant Jesus in Matthew are foreigners from the East. The Magi stand for peoples and cultures beyond the familiar, beyond Judaism, to be sure, but also beyond all narrow definitions of Christendom that we have inherited from the past.

Similarly, our ministry in the Church must reach out, not only geographically and ethnically but beyond other barriers as well. Because our work is specifically oriented toward education, we run a risk of confusing the mission of the Church with academic goals. Our catechetics must be accessible to those who are not academically gifted as well as those who are uncomfortable in a traditional educational mode. Not all children or adults learn alike. It is especially important to be inclusive of the physically and developmentally disabled when we share the faith that has been passed on to us. In their 1995 *Guidelines for Celebration of the Sacraments with Persons with Disabilities*, the U.S. bishops write:

> In accord with canon 777.4, pastors are responsible to be as inclusive as possible in providing evangelization, catechetical formation and sacramental preparation for parishioners with disabilities. . . . Parish catechetical and sacramental preparation programs may need to be adapted for some parishioners with disabilities (#5).

Adaptation is always a challenge. Catechesis with persons with certain disabilities may require special training and the assistance of certain volunteers. It certainly requires a willingness to be flexible and creative.

The overall parish community may also be in need of a challenge. It is the whole community of faith that passes on the faith. Parishes must be open to including those who are excluded in other parts of society. The bishops stress that an open and inclusive attitude of parishioners toward persons with disabilities is necessary in order for the parish to be fully accessible. The work of the DRE may include education for the rest of the parish about this part of the catechetical ministry. As the bishops conclude, "Pastoral ministers are encouraged to develop specific programs aimed at forming a community of believers known for its joyful inclusion of all of God's people around the table of the Lord" (#6).

## PEOPLE OF GOD

In our relationships with people, we must guard against litmus tests for Church participation, whether economic, educational, or even moral. Jesus made it clear often enough that he had come for those who need him, not for the "righteous" or the "healthy who had no need of a physician." No one should be ostracized. The "unteachable" one that we turn away or despair of reaching may well be a modern counterpart to a certain tax collector who found Jesus.

> As Jesus was walking along, he saw a man called Matthew sitting at the tax booth; and he said to him, "Follow me." And he got up and followed him. And as he sat at dinner in the house, many tax collectors and sinners came and were sitting with him and his disciples. When the Pharisees saw this, they said to his disciples, "Why does your teacher eat with tax collectors and sinners?" But when he heard this, he said, "Those who are well have no need of a physician but those who are sick. Go and learn what this means, 'I desire mercy, not sacrifice.' For I have come to call not the righteous but sinners." (Matthew 9:9–13)

That message should be liberating good news for all of us. One of the most debilitating and alienating habits we can fall into is perfectionism. What is so amazing about the Church is that, while each of us individually is indeed sinful, together God has made us into a holy people.

The second chapter of the *Dogmatic Constitution on the Church* reminds us that the "People of God" is not a new concept but really the original design. The chapter begins with a reference to the Acts of the Apostles, from the preaching of St. Peter:

> At all times and among every people, God has given welcome to whosoever fears him and does what is right (cf. Acts 10:35). It has pleased God, however, to make [people] holy and save them not merely as individuals without any mutual bonds but by making them into a single people, a people which acknowledges him in truth and serves him in holiness (#9).

Fortunately, it is not the job of the DRE to judge the holy people of God but to welcome them and to place before their eyes a faith that is centered on Christ.

Later in this same second chapter, "The People of God," the text examines the worldwide nature of this people: "All . . . are called to belong to the new People of God. Wherefore this people, while remaining one and unique, is to be spread throughout the whole world and must exist in all ages" (#13). A little further on we read, "It follows that among all the nations of the Earth there is but one People of God, which takes its citizens from every race. . . . For all the faithful scattered throughout the world are in communion with each other in the Holy Spirit." (#13). The communion of saints is a global reality that we need to contemplate so that it becomes a given in our understanding of the faith and an attitude that forms all of our human and professional relationships.

In the next section, the *Constitution* begins to set forth in detail how all the people of the world are part of the one People of God. The Council Fathers write about the borders or definitions of the Church itself. What is striking is that the borders are presented as permeable. We may use the image of concentric circles, like ripples in a pond, ever expanding to be more inclusive. Thus, by "the Church" is understood all those in union with the "visible structure" of the Catholic Church. The writers then pause to affirm strongly that this union, however, will not afford salvation to anyone who "does not persevere in charity" (#14).

Secondly, all Christians are joined to the Church, even though only in partial union with one another, because of a shared belief in one baptism, reverence for sacred Scripture, and faith in Christ (#15). But even those "who have not yet received the Gospel" are seen as connected to the one People of God in various ways. Specifically mentioned are the Jews, the people from whom Christ was born, and the Moslems, who profess the faith of Abraham. Finally, those who have no knowledge of the Gospel yet seek to serve God, and even those who have no explicit knowledge of God, are included. Special notice is given to "goodness and truth" present in these people (#16).

When we read this text, our understanding of the communion of saints must expand because we hear a message about God's life, God's grace, and God's Holy Spirit present and active even outside the distinct boundaries of theism. For the DRE, then, although most parish tasks will be addressed to inquirers or members of the parish community, there must be an attitude of openness and inclusion, an appreciation of interfaith and ecumenical dialogue, and a willingness to work together with other Christians, persons of other faiths, and persons of no explicit faith. There is much that we share even from such different perspectives. To deny the importance of the common goals and values of religiously diverse communities is to stifle the Holy Spirit and present only a limited and partial view of God's growing reign.

## AN ESCHATOLOGICAL VISION

Lastly, our vision of the Church must be eschatological. Our history points forward to something we do not yet see but hold onto in faith and hope, and work toward in loving service. The Council offers a vision of the totality of the awaited restoration: "Then the human race as well as the entire world, which is intimately related to man and achieves its purpose through him, will be perfectly reestablished in Christ" (*Dogmatic Constitution on the Church*, #48). The Council's words are filled with an optimism that should be a tonic for us, for in the midst of struggles and even groaning, the promised reign of God takes form:

> The final age of the world has already come upon us (cf. 1 Corinthians 10:11). The renovation of the world has been irrevocably decreed and in this age is already anticipated in some real way. For even now on this Earth the Church is marked with a genuine though imperfect holiness. However, until there is a new heaven and a new Earth where justice dwells (cf. 2 Peter 3:13), the pilgrim Church in her sacraments and institutions, which pertain to this present time, takes on the appearance of this passing world. She herself dwells among creatures who groan and travail in pain until now and await the revelation of the sons of God. (#48)

It would be foolish to say that the life and ministry of the parish DRE is without the groaning and travailing and pain that St. Paul saw and that the Second Vatican Council also noticed in the Church. At the end of chapter 6 of this *Constitution*, the Council reaffirms the doctrine of the communion of saints as articulated by the Second Council of Nicea, the Council of Florence, and the Council of Trent. With that, the bishops present themselves as part of a long history, in touch with centuries of reflection on this very comforting "vital fellowship," which is most authentically shown "not so much in the multiplying of external acts, but rather in the intensity of our active love" (#51).

For the DRE, to labor in the parish, to do the work of catechetics, to share the good news of faith in Christ, is to form part of a great choir, reaching back two millennia, with all people, on all the continents of the Earth, and on pilgrimage forward to the coming reign of Christ. We are not alone. We can take courage as St. Paul did: "Therefore, since we are surrounded by so great a cloud of witnesses, let us also lay aside every weight and the sin that clings so closely, and let us run with perseverance the race that is set before us . . . . [Then we shall] not grow weary or lose heart" (Hebrews 12:1–3).

**FOR REFLECTION:**

1. What period in the history of the Church do you think has the most to say to our own age? Do you see parallels with the conflicts and issues that concern the Church today? How was the work you do in the parish handled at other times in the Church's history? Who did this work? Can you choose one Church leader from another century who might be a role model for you?

2. Consider the various ethnic groups in your parish or diocese. How do they relate to one another? How does your ministry take into account the social and cultural backgrounds of these diverse people? What steps might you take to make the global reality of the Church more

visible to people in your parish? What do you need to learn about the people in your parish in order to be more sensitive to their traditions and needs?

3. Does your personal faith and spirituality have an eschatological dimension? How do you balance the Gospel call to service and justice in the present with the knowledge that the true reign of peace and justice is yet to come? What are some ways you can include a hope-filled vision of the reign of God in religious education for children, youth, and adults? How do you understand the relationship between the Church and God's reign?

# Conclusion

The vocation and the ministry of the DRE, as we have seen, is complex and involves maintaining a careful balance. We need to be sensitive to our own needs for growth even as we strive to attend to the needs of others. Those needs themselves are multifaceted: spiritual, emotional, intellectual, physical. We hope that this booklet has helped you not only appreciate the challenge presented but has also helped you recognize how many of the ordinary events and circumstances in the life of the DRE can actually be turned into resources for maintaining one's balance and perspective. In a real sense, we will find God in the "details" once we learn to be attentive to them. Ultimately, it is by recognizing God's presence in all that we do that we will find the energy and guidance to enrich others even as we become enriched ourselves.

# Selected Bibliography

## PRIMARY SOURCES

The following short list constitutes the minimum basic list of documents with which the parish DRE should be familiar. In addition, collections of papal encyclicals, Council decrees and canons, and statements by the U.S. bishops and the local bishop should be easily accessible.

*Catechism of the Catholic Church.* Chicago: Loyola Press, 1994.

*Go and Make Disciples: A National Plan and Strategy for Catholic Evangelization in the United States.* Washington: USCC, 1992.

*Holman Bible Dictionary for Windows,* Version 1.0g. Parsons Technology, 1994.

*Rite of Christian Initiation of Adults.* Chicago: Liturgy Training Publications, 1988.

*Sharing the Light of Faith: National Catechetical Directory for Catholics of the United States.* Washington: USCC, 1978.

*The Documents of Vatican II.* Walter M. Abbott, S.J., ed. New York: Herder and Herder, 1966.

*The Holy Bible.* New Revised Standard Version. Nashville: Thomas Nelson Publishers, 1989.

*The Code of Canon Law.* Grand Rapids, MI: Eerdmans, 1983.

## OTHER MATERIALS

Barry, William A., and William G. Connolly. *The Practice of Spiritual Direction.* San Francisco: Harper SF, 1982.

Harris, Maria. *The D.R.E. Book: Questions and Strategies for Parish Personnel.* New York: Paulist, 1976. Although the role of the DRE has unfolded significantly since this book was published, Harris' insights into procedures, models of leadership, and ministerial relationships remain valid.

*John Paul II, Catechist: The Text with Commentary and Discussion Questions of Catechesi Tradendae, the Pope's New Charter for Religious Education Today.* Chicago: Franciscan Herald Press, 1980.

Moran, Gabriel. *Religious Education Development: Images for the Future.* Minneapolis: Winston Press, 1983. This study discusses what has been learned in the psychological professions about educational development at various ages of life, bringing that knowledge into dialogue with religious and moral development.

Nouwen, Henri J. M. *The Wounded Healer.* Garden City, NY: Image Books, 1979. This is a classic spiritual reflection on the nature of ministry and the person of the minister.

O'Hare, Padraic. *The Way of Faithfulness: Contemplation and Formation in the Church.* Valley Forge, PA: Trinity Press International, 1993. This extraordinary book is a profound presentation of the necessity of authentic contemplation at the heart of the enterprise of religious education. The reader will see the ministry of the religious educator with wholly new eyes.

O'Hare, Padraic, ed. *Keeping PACE: 25 Years of Theology, Education, and Ministry from PACE.* Dubuque, IA: Brown-ROA, 1996. This is a collection of articles from a publication exclusively addressed to religious educators on a broad spectrum of issues in religious education. Featuring outstanding writers in their fields, PACE has been an invaluable resource for many DREs. This collection represents the best of the best.

Pennington, M. Basil. *Called: New Thinking on Christian Vocation.* New York: Seabury, 1983. Primarily written from the point of view of monastic life, this book has much to say about Christian vocation in general.

Sanford, John A. *Ministry Burnout.* Louisville: Westminster John Knox, 1992.

Sweetser, Thomas, S. J., and Carol Wisniewski Holden. *Leadership in a Successful Parish.* San Francisco: Harper and Row, 1987. This book discusses the various roles and tasks of the parish team, providing a good analysis of structural dynamics in the community.

Whitehead, James D., and Evelyn Eaton. *Method in Ministry: Theological Reflection and Christian Ministry.* New York: Seabury, 1980. Not a how-to book on doing ministry but a book on thinking about it theologically. This book may be valuable in introducing the underpinnings of theological reflection, especially where preparation for religious education ministry has been largely practical.

NOTES